THE CITY IS A LABYRINTH

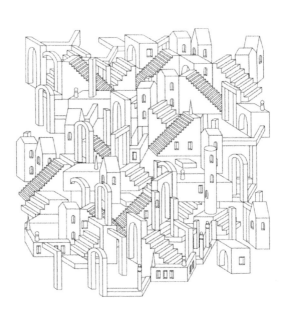

THE CITY IS
A LABYRINTH

a walking guide for urban animists

Sarah Kate Istra Winter

Directions

Before Embarking..1

First Steps...9

Betwixt and Between.................................21

Let's Get Lost...27

Where the Wild Things Are 32

Ways and Means 42

Further Exploration.................................57

Your Guide..59

For all the vibrant spirits of Eugene, Oregon—from the wooded parks and flowing waterways to the alleys and abandoned lots—your powerful presence has made every exploration a worthwhile adventure.

Before Embarking

IT IS EASY TO BE AN ANIMIST IN A FOREST.
The natural world is alive with spiritual energy.
Healing plants sprout from the earth. Powerful,
totemic animals make their homes in burrows and
branches. Messages can be read in the stars above,
or the discovery of a meaningfully shaped rock.
Every foray into the wilderness can bear spiritual
and magical fruit in the form of insights, omens,
small exchanges of goodwill with the local wights,
even transformative encounters with gods.

But most of us don't live in the forest, or
anywhere near one. We live and work—and pray
and worship—in cities, from modest urban

settings to sprawling metropolises. More people live in cities now than ever before and this trend seems likely to continue as our population keeps growing. Yet, many polytheists and animists still think of the spiritual world as something only, or primarily, accessible in nature.

Of course, a truly animist perspective holds everything as sacred, and knows that spirits are everywhere. And close observation of even the most urbanized environment will reveal an active ecosystem, and even uncover some pockets of unspoiled nature flourishing amidst the concrete and steel. But the city is more than just an echo of—or cage for—the spiritual power of the natural world. For those attuned to the right currents, the city holds Mysteries of its own.

Polytheism has always been rooted in Place. It involves a complex web of relationships that is shaped not only by the individual and their community, but by the land itself, the spirits encountered every day, and the unique forms the gods take in that place. Local spirits, especially, are an incredibly important and powerful force in the lives of indigenous polytheists and animists, and should be so for those of us adopting this religious mindset. They are just as involved—if not more so—as the gods in such human concerns as health, climate, fertility (of body and land), personal luck, wealth, and spiritual development. They are indispensible allies when attempting to influence events by magical means. They often also act as a bridge to the gods Themselves.

Such local spirits are not only found in pristine natural environments; they are everywhere, including our cities. Some are of the same types familiar from forest and river and field (especially when the forests and rivers and fields are found within urban boundaries), while others are unique to the city itself—spirits of buildings and bridges, of highways and public squares. Gods, too, can be found here, and many gods even have special affinities for urban sites and activities.

Contrary to common misperception, the city is not antithetical or inhospitable to polytheism or animism. One has only to look at some of the great cities of antiquity for examples of thriving urban polytheist practice—ancient Athens or Alexandria, for instance. Or in modern times, observe the success of Shinto shrines in Tokyo, or the way Afro-Caribbean diasporic traditions have flourished in New York City, Miami and Los Angeles. In fact, cities themselves are often recognized as possessing a *genius loci* (spirit of place), acknowledged even by monotheists and atheists in some fashion, and represented by potent symbolic landmarks. (The most overtly animist example that comes to mind is the statue of Portlandia—a copper, trident-wielding goddess perched atop a building in downtown Portland, Oregon.)

As urban animists and polytheists, it is imperative that we establish a meaningful relationship with our local environment just as we would if we lived on a working farm or in the deep woods or on a seaside cliff. But it's hard to do this if your only experience of your city is mediated through a barrier of glass and steel travelling at fifty miles per hour, or if you never venture beyond the safe and familiar confines of your home, workplace and nearest shops. To deeply

4

engage with the spirit of the city, and the *spirits* within it, it is necessary to put foot to pavement and WALK.

"I walk everywhere, rejecting the internal combustion engine as an effete surrender to laziness and the ignoble advantage of convenience."

– Guy Davenport, *The Geography of the Imagination*

Walking is slow—one of the reasons it's almost always rejected as a form of transportation in favor of bicycles, cars, trains, etc. But it is precisely this slowness that allows you the time to pay attention, to notice what (and Who) is around you. Travelling at walking pace means, quite literally, being able to stop and smell the roses—or more importantly, perhaps, the native wildflowers growing through the cracks in the pavement. It means listening to birdsong, or overhearing a chance bit of conversation while passing a café. It means having the time to let your thoughts unwind, your mind wander along with your feet. It means making room for magic to happen, and space for the gods to appear.

Cities—especially in the United States—have become increasingly hostile to foot traffic, consistently forgoing or even removing pedestrian access in favor of convenience for vehicles. Our mainstream culture promotes consumerism and constant distraction, and encourages speedy travel between the places where we make money and the places where we spend it. But just by being aware of the gods and valuing the sacred, we are challenging this way of life. In such a context, walking becomes a statement of resistance, an assertion of our priorities. It not only practically but symbolically complements an urban spiritual practice.

We are not entirely treading on new ground here. By walking through the city with religious and/or magical intent, we are perhaps expanding on the idea of the dérive (meaning "drifting"), that playful, purposely aimless wandering developed by the

Situationists (heirs of the Surrealists), which could result in uncanny synchronicity. It was in a sense its own art form, albeit an ephemeral one. A dérive was not undertaken in order to go from one set point to another, but rather to discover, to become delightfully disoriented, to connect to the city in new ways. This practice in turn contributed to the development of psycho-geography—a field which explores the emotional and behavioral impact of place in an urban context, through direct, experiential methods, usually on foot. Studying these concepts can inform our own practice, and suggest a kind of animist dérive, which might use similar methods but with a more overtly metaphysical approach.

"[Psychogeographers] share a perception of the city as a site of mystery and seek to reveal the true nature that lies beneath the flux of the everyday."

– Merlin Coverley, *Psychogeography*

Once you embrace the city as a spiritual setting it its own right, and begin to view it with one eye in the otherworlds, you will find a special and potent magic there. Streets that may only serve as a frustrating maze when trying to find the nearest ATM can become the winding route of a labyrinth when traversed in a mystical mindset. Within this labyrinth are strange, surprising creatures, un-imagined secrets, new faces of old gods. You will find just as many messages, insights and encounters as in the forest described at the outset of this chapter, but some may come in very different guises. No journey will ever be quite the same as another, no matter how many times you walk the same path—though, as in the forest, some of the best experiences will be found on unfamiliar paths.

So let us begin to explore.

First Steps

ONE OF THE BEST THINGS ABOUT WALKING in urban spaces as a spiritual practice is that you can start immediately, without any prior knowledge, experience, or fancy tools—though all of those things can enhance your practice as you deepen into it. It is as simple (and sometimes as tremendously difficult) as just paying attention.

The most important thing, especially at first, is to be present in the moment and maintain mindfulness as you walk. To be able to "hear" (literally or metaphorically) the voices of the myriad spirits around you, first you must shut up. That means leave your devices at home (or if you feel you must have them for emergencies, at least turn them off so you are not interrupted, distracted, or tempted to use them for purposes of navigation or other information). You must engage with tangible, physical reality before you can readily access the realms of spirit that are attached to the physical world. Let yourself return to a more natural mental state, where your awareness rests in your immediate environment rather than what is happening with other people in other places. Instead of automatically taking a photograph of something interesting, try drawing it, recording your impressions of it in a notebook, committing the image to memory—or simply enjoying it in the moment and then letting it go. Resist the urge to share your experiences in order to validate them; remember that you are already sharing a meaningful experience with the gods and spirits that are present around you.

So to begin, try walking slowly for just a few blocks in any direction starting from your home—even if you've made this trip a hundred times—and really pay attention to everything you encounter. What plants, animals, and insects are present? What types of building do you pass? Are there any bodies of water nearby? What is the weather like? How many intersections do you go through?

Now, place what you are seeing into a spiritual context. There are several ways to do this. On the most basic animistic level, all of the elements of the environment can be understood and approached as Persons in their own right, from the trees to the birds to the traffic lights. Look around you and try to perceive that you are surrounded by ensouled beings. How does that change the way you conduct yourself?

Of course, even if you believe that all things, alive or not, have a spirit, some are clearly more cohesive, aware, and/or responsive than others—these are the types we usually mean when we use the terms "spirit" or "wight." Such spirits can be placed in a loose taxonomy which can be further tailored to an urban setting.

There are spirits of the local animals, plants,

fungi and minerals, both individually and collectively (often spoken of as a "grandfather/ mother" spirit). In a city, the most prevalent animal spirits might not be the commonly favored totems like Wolf, Bear and Eagle, but rather those of Rat, Raccoon and Pigeon. Power plants might be what some call weeds. These are nonetheless spirits worth knowing and honoring, and can be powerful allies.

Then there are the spirits of features of the landscape, which in a city includes manmade structures like roads, bridges, and buildings, but also rivers, hills, small woodlands, etc. Sometimes you will encounter a spirit who appears to be indistinguishable from the physical feature—the river itself—but you may also find spirits that are closely tied to, but not synonymous with, it— nymphs, for instance, who live on the river's bank.

A particularly strong category of spirits in the city is often the dead, especially the collective dead found in cemeteries. Nearly every city, small or large, has at least one graveyard, often containing early settlers, local heroes, and other honored dead. You might also encounter the presence of dead souls at battle sites, in old houses, in hospitals, near memorials, or just wandering the places they knew in life.

Finally, there are those spirits we can loosely term "fairies"—sometimes overlapping with both spirits of place and the dead—which encompass many different types with countless variations in nature, proclivities, appearance, etc. While some of these eschew dense human settlement (and, in the case of some Celtic fairies at least, the iron that comes with it), plenty seem to still find a home somewhere inside urban boundaries. *

As you take your first short, experimental walks, look out for signs of such spirits. If you can sense Them naturally or have had training in some form of spirit-work or mysticism, this will be relatively easy and simply a matter, again, of paying attention, and learning the unique forms They may take in the city, and in your city specifically. If not, however, you can start by identifying which types of places are likely to have strong spirits (the most prominent natural feature, for instance, or the oldest cemetery, or a huge oak tree, or well-used

---

* For more on the taxonomy outlined here, see my article "A Typology of Spirits" in the Summer 2015 issue ("Building Regional Cultus") of *Walking the Worlds*.

bridge). It is also worth noting areas that have a powerful effect on you emotionally. As you continue to engage with your local environment, you will find that some spots seem to be more conducive to spiritual experiences. And, once you begin to respond to these numinous places (with offerings, prayer, magic) and build relationships, you will further hone your ability to recognize the spirits around you.

In addition to all these spirits, there are gods in the city as well. Gods have been associated with, and patrons of, urban communities from the very beginning—sometimes even lending Their names, such as ancient Athens, a city under Athene's protection. And many gods have special interest in and power over aspects of human activity that are prevalent in cities—education, commerce, transportation. But more broadly, the gods can be found almost anywhere.

As you walk, try a little exercise of seeing the gods in everything. To use the Greek pantheon as an example: if you see an oak tree, or get caught in a thunderstorm, there is Zeus; if you pass a liquor store or a theatre, there is Dionysos; pigeons are a type of dove, sacred to Aphrodite; and any time three roads meet they become a *trioditis*, a place to meet Hekate.

You might also find familiar gods manifesting unique, localized aspects in your city, especially if you maintain long-term cultus for Them there. This is also attested to in antiquity. Just as there was Poseidon of Sounion, with His particular holy place and rites, so might there develop a Poseidon of Boston or San Francisco (the latter being especially appropriate, given the earthquake activity there).

Since we are not just talking about urban forms of polytheism but specifically the practice of walking, it should be mentioned that there are several gods who are Themselves wanderers and would be very appropriate patrons of this practice, most notably Hermes, Mercury and Odin.

Hermes (and His Roman counterpart Mercury) is a messenger god, a guide of souls, always on the move between our world, the abode of the gods, and the realm of the dead, with His herald's rod and winged boots. Travelers would often build stone piles at crossroads in His honor, which eventually became the well-known carved pillars called herms; these functioned as milestones and boundary markers.

Odin is called Vegtam (Way-tamer or Wanderer) and moves between all the nine worlds, recognized by His broad-brimmed hat and walking staff. He seeks knowledge and power wherever it may be.

If so inclined, beginning your walks with prayers to any of these deities (or others with similar natures), or incorporating Them in more comprehensive ways into the process, would be potentially quite powerful. They know all the hidden ways, and might be petitioned as guides, with the right offerings.

"Betwixt and between
The seen and unseen
Pathways of spirit and gravel
He of the lost souls
The gaps and the crossroads
Hail to the great god of travel"

– song for Hermes by Fawnn

Speaking of offerings, they are an important part of these walks, and there will be suggestions later on for specific offerings you can bring with you, but when you first start out, it might be easiest to focus on those offerings you can make anywhere, with nothing on hand. This is partly so that you don't get overwhelmed before even beginning, thinking that you have to have the perfect set of items, and partly to emphasize that this can be done anywhere at any time, with no special preparation.

One of the most potent and meaningful gifts you can always give is your breath. This is, in a very real way, your life force. An easy way to make breath into an offering is through song—or more simply, even intoning a single note. If you know any songs or chants—especially those with spiritual meaning for you—try singing them as you walk (or, write one for this express purpose if you wish). Breathwork and singing can also induce altered states of consciousness, which may enhance your walk—this will be returned to later. If you smoke, casually or ritually, you can also use breath to blow burnt tobacco or other herbs into the air or towards a particular object as an offering. Another simple form of on-the-go worship is to make a hand gesture or movement indicating respect and honor. For instance, the motion we know as "blowing a kiss" was a method of prayer in antiquity. Finally, check what you have in your pockets—a few coins, a small piece of a granola bar, a drop of perfume, can all suffice in a pinch.

Prayer and offerings are the ways we speak to the gods and spirits, but They also speak to us. While ways to use divination on city walks will be explored, for now just keep an eye out for omens that can be read easily in your environment. Sometimes these appear as literal signs—a billboard whose message seems spookily relevant at that moment. Other times you might see a marking in the shape of a rune, or notice an animal acting unusually (the activity of birds especially has long been used for this purpose). The more you open your eyes and ears to messages from the otherworlds, the more you will become part of the vast, magical conversation that is always going on all around you.

It might be useful to limit yourself to just these first small but important steps when starting a practice of urban spirit-walking, before you start assembling special tools, exploring specific numinous places, planning ritual acts, or researching local history (all of which will become important eventually). Spend some time just learning the art of spiritually-oriented mindfulness as you walk a short distance around the familiar areas of your city. Perhaps even experiment with making a mundane excursion to the corner store or post office into a spirit-walk, just by paying attention, practicing recognizing the spirits and gods you encounter, and maybe making a small offering or prayer.

A final note: It is usually best to walk alone. Solitude allows you the mental silence necessary to start tuning in to what is happening around you on a spiritual level. It also means you can respond to whatever calling or gut instinct you feel to go in a different direction, act in a certain way, etc. Outside of special circumstances (like festival processions), this usually works best as a solitary practice. However, it is possible to have a companion on your journeys if they are someone you share a close spiritual affinity with, and who understands the purpose and nature of the practice. Sometimes this can even enhance the experience, as you will have someone with whom you can confirm impressions, share knowledge, and build local cultus together.

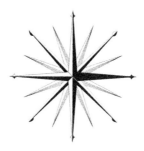

Betwixt and Between

ALL BY ITSELF, THE ACT OF WALKING PUTS you in a liminal state—neither here nor there but in between. This makes it especially suitable for spiritual and mystical purposes, where we are already seeking to draw back the veil between the worlds for a moment and interact with the gods and spirits.

Walking can be a prayer in motion, a way of using our physical bodies to connect and communicate with the divine, just like yogic asanas or sacred dance are. Walking can be an offering, an expenditure of time, energy, and focus given freely—even more so when a long, challenging journey is undertaken. (An especially ambitious walk over a great distance to a particularly significant destination may even become a pilgrimage.) Walking can be an autonomous ritual—for instance, acting out the story of Demeter's search for Persephone, as the initiates did on their long walk to Eleusis from Athens in ancient Greece. It can also be part of a larger festival or holy day, consisting of a grand pro-cession to a sacred place where a more elaborate ritual will occur. Walking can be meditation, as the Buddhists sometimes use it, a time of quiet reflection or empty-mindedness, a slowing down, narrowing the attention to breath and movement.

And walking can be a catalyst for altered states of consciousness—the rhythmic steps, quickened heartbeat, change in breathing, even the sunlight flickering between the leaves of trees can serve as a trigger for trance, especially for those already inclined to mystic states. Walking in the city while in an altered headspace can be difficult and even outright dangerous, so caution must be taken. Not all areas are appropriate for such an experience; it is impossible to safely navigate busy intersections or dodge large groups of fellow pedestrians while in a trance. But if you can find a quiet neighborhood, an empty park—or even better, a pocket of wilderness within the city—and are able to keep at least one part of your mind attentive to the physical world, it can be a powerful practice. In an altered state of consciousness, it becomes much easier to recognize numinous spots, and more likely that you will directly encounter local spirits (or at least, that you will be able to perceive Them). You can also better perform divination or magic, and receive messages from the gods.

To take this a step further, if you are already experienced and comfortable with trancework, you might begin to explore the practice of pathwalking.* This is a method of operating in both worlds at once—the material and the spiritual. You move around in physical reality while simultaneously peeling back the veil a bit and experiencing a Place on the other side, via an altered state of consciousness. It is not something

---

* See *The Pathwalker's Guide to the Nine Worlds* by Raven Kaldera for more on this practice; although placed squarely in a Heathen worldview, it contains useful instructions that can be used in almost any tradition.

everyone can do, and it takes a toll on the body and mind, but it allows you a more immersive experience of the otherworlds than can be accessed by faring forth in spirit alone. When practiced repeatedly in the same places (usually those where the veil is already thin), it can even strengthen the connections between the physical land and its spiritual counterpart, and this works just as much in cities as out in nature. This can bring greater vitality and potency to the location on this side, as well as providing you a more open point of entry to the otherworlds.

In my book *Between the Worlds*, I described a useful technique for learning the trick of path-walking which I think of as "narrowed focus"—this was actually developed on urban spirit-walks and bears repeating here:

The simplest version can be done by paying attention only to your feet as you walk along. Narrow your field of vision until you can only see your feet and the surface on which you are walking—the sidewalk, the forest path, whatever it may be. It helps if you can also narrow your other senses, so that, for instance, you predominantly are hearing only your own footsteps rather than any distant noises that would alert you to what is happening in the larger area.

In this little bubble, you are still experiencing physical reality, but it is somewhat separated from the world that you know is around you. This helps you both to disconnect a little bit from the tyranny of your preconceived ideas (what you have come to expect about your surroundings), and to access other Places which might look very similar from that limited viewpoint. For instance, if you are walking down a city street and look only at the asphalt and concrete and grass around your feet, you could be almost anywhere—across the country, across the world, or even in another world entirely. You could be in the present day or in a moment that happened decades ago. You could be alone or surrounded by others. The familiar suddenly becomes the unknown, and that disorientation creates an opportunity for you to slip sideways a little, into a liminal state where both Here and There exist together.

Once you feel that altered perception taking hold, you can slowly raise your head and start to shift your attention to the rest of the world around you, seeing it all with new eyes. You may literally see the otherworld superimposed on this one, if you have that gift, or you may experience the dual realities in other ways—for instance, encountering unusual objects or people that are clearly being influenced by spiritual forces, hearing strange music or a voice just out of sight, feeling compelled to take a certain route that leads you to a significant location or event, etc.

Of course, there is some practical danger in this technique, especially when done in an urban environment. Taking your eyes off your surroundings, even for a few minutes, puts you at risk in a number of ways, so it must only be done in certain situations. But if done carefully, it can be a very powerful tool.

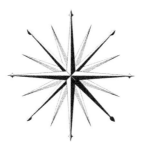

Let's Get Lost

THERE ARE TWO BASIC APPROACHES TO urban spirit-walks. The first, which will be discussed in detail in the following chapter, is destination-based. This is probably the easier and more familiar approach for most people, as we usually set out on any journey—in city or wilderness, on foot or by vehicle—with a specific location as our goal. And it is an important and effective way to explore the animistic landscape, by identifying and visiting those places of special power, interest or significance.

But the other method is perhaps especially

suited to the urban environment, and that is the aimless wander with no destination in mind. This is the dérive of the Situationists, who encouraged their members to shun the familiar when abroad in the city, to choose their path randomly, to let the city itself guide them. It is an approach that also works well for the magically-inclined, as it allows for moments of deeply meaningful synchronicity and discovery. When you are not bound to any route, and make your way by some combination of chance, instinct and divination, it makes room for the gods and spirits to influence your experience, either directly or indirectly.

"More conservative minds deprive coincidence of meaning by treating it as background noise or garbage, but the shape-shifting mind pesters the distinction between accident and essence and remakes this world out of whatever happens. At its obsessive extreme such attention is the beginning of paranoia (all coincidence makes 'too much sense'), but in a more capacious mind it is a kind of happy genius, ready to make music out of other people's noise."

– Lewis Hyde, *Trickster Makes This World*

This is easiest to do in an unfamiliar city, of course. And while this book is largely meant to bring you into a closer engagement with the spirits of your home environment, most of the concepts and techniques can also be applied when you travel. Numinous places and local spirits are worth discovering and visiting anywhere, and exploring a new city in this way—rather than seeing the usual tourist attractions—is much more interesting and rewarding.

Back on your home turf, however, you may have to exert more effort to escape the familiar, especially if you have lived there for many years. Still, it is worth letting yourself get lost from time to time. You can most easily do this by taking some form of transportation to a part of the city that is unknown to you, and beginning your walk from there. But you may also be surprised to find that you don't know your own neighborhood as well as you think, once you veer off the well-trodden paths.

Try walking along streets you've only driven down previously, and you might experience them entirely differently, and see things you missed when travelling at a much faster pace. Turn right

29

where you usually turn left and see where it takes you. Walk through alleys and behind buildings. Go to an area at night that you've only been to during daylight—it's amazing how much the darkness changes a place. It's quite possible to have an adventure right in your own backyard, so to speak.

"Not to find one's way around a city does not mean much. But to lose one's way in a city, as one loses one's way in a forest, requires some schooling. Street names must speak to the urban wanderer like the snapping of dry twigs, and little streets in the heart of the city must reflect the times of day, for him, as clearly as a mountain valley."

—Walter Benjamin, *Berlin Childhood around 1900*

Note that you can utilize altered states of consciousness—or even really diligent mindfulness—to see even the most familiar places as if for the first time. Trance states are also quite conducive to a spirit-led, destination-less wandering, wherever you are (while again, taking proper caution to ensure your safety).

Even if you mostly engage in purposeful, planned spirit-walks to build relationships with your local environment, be sure to go on a good, messy ramble now and again. (This is one of those instances where having a kindred spirit along for the journey can greatly enhance the experience.) Remember that while devotional and magical practice is certainly serious and holy work, it can also be exciting, enchanting, and fun.

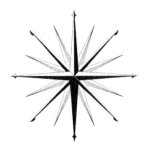

Where the Wild Things Are

EVEN IN THE MOST URBAN ENVIRONMENTS, spirits are present. And no matter how inter-twined with our manmade routes and edifices, these Persons (in the animistic view) are still very much other-than-human. They are likely to have different desires, needs, priorities, preferences and rules of conduct—different from ours, and different from each other's as well. Make no assumptions—most importantly perhaps, do not assume that They want you there. As you start exploring your city and hoping to forge relation-ships with the wights there, remember that not all of Them will be receptive to your overtures, or even your presence. Pay attention to any signs that you may not be wanted—including a sudden feeling of fear (perhaps Pan's panic, as it were), revulsion, or dread—and do not ignore the urge to vacate the premises. Also note areas of consistent trouble over time—the kind that manifests in the mundane world—such as failed shops, violence, and pollution; these can often indicate the presence of hostile wights, either as a result, or perhaps the cause, of such problems. If your path to a place is physically barred or hindered, perform divination to ascertain if you should go elsewhere instead. Plenty of spirits *will* welcome your attention and devotion, and it's best for everyone if you find and focus on those.

"From the dérive point of view cities have a psychogeographical relief with constant currents, fixed points and vortexes which strongly discourage entry into or exit from certain zones."

– Guy Debord, *Theory of the Dérive*

When dealing with any spirits you encounter, including those you become familiar or even friendly with, always maintain proper etiquette. What does that entail? If you know the cultural provenance of a given wight, that will be your best guide—treating Them in the manner prescribed by Their home culture is usually a safe approach. Nymphs are going to want certain rites and offerings that may not work as well with alfar—though you may find that certain types of spirit are similar regardless of origin. Most polytheistic peoples knew of dangerous spirits who lurk in bodies of water, for instance, waiting to drown the unwary passerby—if you encounter such a creature (or just notice the hair on the back of your neck rise as you approach a murky pond), it would be best to leave immediately, and it doesn't really matter if it was a rusalka or a kelpie.

If you aren't sure Who you're dealing with or what They want, try following fairy tale rules. Always be polite, courteous, and honest. Help those in need, and repay any help you are given. Ask permission to take anything, and leave a gift in exchange when you do. Keep your promises. Share what you have. Rely on your allies for assistance. And always pay attention to signs, and to your gut feelings. Remember that it's not all about you. Honoring the spirits of place starts with respect.

So where do you start looking for these wild, wonderful wights, and how do you identify numinous places?

First you might want to locate the major natural features—even in urban landscapes, these are important and likely to be home to powerful spirits if not gods. Perhaps your city lies at the confluence of two rivers, or in the shadow of a majestic mountain. Research the last animistic culture that lived in your area and discover their holy places (if you're lucky, you may even learn some old names or traditional offerings). You might be surprised to find an ancient place of power is now right in the middle of the city. Of course, if you are in Europe, you will find some cities that were built by polytheists, where remains from the ancient religion are more obvious. (In

North America, some non-native animists hesitate to adopt or adapt anything from the indigenous traditions, fearing the offense of cultural appropriation. But if done carefully and respectfully, it is actually important and proper to honor the spirits of one's land as They have been honored in the past, and taking the time to learn about that and use it as a basis for building new relationships is a sign of reverence. Certainly one should not neglect native spirits due to political concerns.)

Look for smaller oases of nature within the landscape of steel and concrete—parks are the most obvious and ubiquitous, and in some cities can be large and wooded enough to almost be considered forests (Portland's eponymous Forest Park is the best example of this). Pay attention to especially large or unusual single trees as well, including those lining the streets in any part of the city, and especially any marked as "heritage trees." Visit all bodies of water—rivers, lakes, ponds, creeks, streams, and even manmade ones like mill races and reservoirs. Fountains are often occupied by a spirit, and both fountains and wells have been important places of worship since antiquity in many cultures.

Note the difference in atmosphere and character between created natural spaces like parks, golf courses, institutional grounds, playing fields, and gardens, and those wilder natural sites which have been enclosed by the growth of the city—wetlands, riparian zones, woodlands, meadows, etc. Both can be sacred, but they tend to have very different "moods" and be home to different sorts of spirits.

Do a little research on the history of your city at the library or historical society, to find places relevant for exploration (as well as to give yourself a deeper overall understanding of the city, which might assist in strengthening your spiritual connection to it). Historical landmarks might lead you to places of great age and power, or sites of significant events you would wish to mark. Statues and other monuments honoring city founders or famous past denizens can be used for hero cultus, as can their graves. And cemeteries in general are good places to honor the dead who built and shaped and loved your city (and are often beautiful natural areas in themselves). You might also encounter roadside shrines, ghost bikes, and other memorial markers appropriate as offering sites.

"And sometimes in my attempts to steer homewards, upon nautical principles, by fixing my eye on the pole-star, and seeking ambitiously for a north-west passage, instead of circumnavigating all the capes and headlands I had doubled in my outward voyage, I came suddenly upon such knotty problems of alleys, such enigmatical entries, and such sphinx's riddles of streets without thoroughfares, as must, I conceive, baffle the audacity of porters, and confound the intellects of hackney-coachmen. I could almost have believed, at times, that I must be the first discoverer of some of these *terrae incognitae*, and doubted, whether they had yet been laid down in the modern charts of London."

– Thomas De Quincey,
Confessions of an English Opium-Eater

An especially useful exercise is identifying liminal places, both on a physical and spiritual level (though these are often the same, following the principle of "as above, so below"). These include crossroads (from dirt paths to busy intersections), narrow strips of woodland between or behind populated areas, running water, old disused tracks, alleys, industrial wastelands, storm drains (great for chthonic work), abandoned buildings, and the very edges of the city proper. Some liminal places aren't outwardly obvious, but can be sensed by those sensitive to areas where the veil between the worlds is thinner.

Don't neglect indoor spaces in your search for the numinous. Stairwells and basements can be just as liminal as crossroads. Sometimes important historical places are inside buildings, and some buildings are naturally associated with gods (a post office for Hermes, university for Athene, court-house for Dike, hospital for Asklepios, etc.). Certain indoor spaces have an inherent element of randomness that makes them particularly suitable for a magical adventure and invites interaction with gods and spirits in the form of omens and chance encounters: libraries, museums, galleries, flea markets, thrift stores, used bookstores. Try asking the gods to lead you to a meaningful find in any of these places (just be careful not to let your spirit-walk turn into a mundane shopping trip).

As you explore, note place names, and what they reveal or suggest historically, environmentally, and folklorically. Most cities have streets named after trees, for instance, which may help you find a certain type of dryad, or an appropriate place for a deity offering (Alder Street for Bran, etc.). When you are researching the city's past, also note any meaningful historical names for areas that may have since changed—sometimes these can lead you to a potent spot, or even become a more appropriate name to use as you build an animistic relationship there. You may also, over time, decide to re-name places of special significance to you with more magical or meaningful titles.

Some places are inherently special and alive with spiritual energy, but numinous spots can be created, too. You may find that over time, if you return to a particular area again and again—make offerings to the spirits there, perform rituals and magic—that it will grow more powerful under your care and attention. You are, after all, feeding and strengthening the wights with such actions, and perhaps even contributing a small portion of your own spirit.

As you deepen into a localized practice, you will find that a walk through the city can become not just an exploration or adventure, but a revisitation of old friends and allies, a remembrance of past spiritual encounters. Not only will the urban landscape come alive, it will be marked with uniquely personal sites. You are creating the map to accompany your own sacred Story.

Ways and Means

GOING ON INTENTIONAL WALKS AS A means of discovering and honoring the spirits of place in a city can take myriad forms. Initially, it might be best to experiment with as many variables as possible as you craft a practice best suited to your religious inclinations and your local wights. Of course, you must also take into consideration the physical characteristics of the city in question—spirit-walks will look different in a small college town than a large metropolis, or one with plentiful pedestrian paths versus one where cars are the assumed default mode of transportation.

Don't hesitate to play with this practice, as it can (and should) be enjoyable and even exciting as much as it is serious and devotional. Take long, exhausting treks through the city, and short, simple jaunts to nearby spots. Wander without purpose sometimes for an hour or two in any direction, but also try some focused walks to specific, special places which you research and plan in advance. Walk at different times of day—you may find you encounter certain spirits only at dawn, or after dark, or in the bright sun of midday. (Dusk is a particularly potent, liminal time to be in a state of motion.) Walk the same routes in each season so that you become familiar with the changes to the environment over a year, which are often reflected in the spiritual world as well. Walk in all kinds of weather—look for water wights rejoicing in the rain, or feel the dread power of the Host who accompany a fierce windstorm.

In addition to regular wandering rambles and places you visit repeatedly to build up cultus, try some thematic walks. These are great for seeing a city through different lenses, and also may bring you unexpected insights and experiences. Walk along communication systems (following phone lines, or a postal route), transportation systems (train tracks, bike paths, canals), or water infrastructure (tracing the course of your drinking water, or walking from a river's source to its appearance in the center of the city). Visit places where food is grown or raised within city limits (urban farms, backyard chicken coops, community gardens), and make offerings there to gods of agriculture and fertility. Look up the location of all the Little Free Libraries in town and make a pilgrimage to each one, carrying along religious books to donate or asking the gods to lead you to a meaningful volume. Go on a search for a specific type of flower, or count all the oaks from your house to the nearest park. Plan a route with historical significance, or seek out the oldest street, building or bridge.

It can be particularly rewarding to embark on a series of related and meaningful walks over a longer period of time, as a devotional act. For instance, visit every cemetery in your city over the course of a year and leave flowers on the oldest grave in each. Or take a month to make offerings to the river from every bridge. If you're trying to get closer to a new god or pantheon, this can also be a good way to further that process while simultaneously connecting Them to your immediate environment, so that you create localized worship right from the start. For instance, for Aphrodite you could embark on a series of walks to a variety of locations associated with Her attributes—rose garden, ocean pier, popular proposal spot—taking the opportunity to understand Her better with each journey, and noting if you feel Her presence more strongly in any particular place, suggesting perhaps a site for future rituals and communion.

"The maze-walker, we could say, is a navigator; the labyrinthine path follower a wayfarer. In the carrying on of the wayfarer, every destination is by the way; his path runs always in between. The movements of the navigator, by contrast, are point-to-point, and every point has been arrived at, by calculation, even before setting off towards it."

– Tim Ingold, *The Life of Lines*

Unless you are taking a very specific route on purpose, most walks will have some degree of variability regarding the way you get from Point A to Point B (and of course, the dérive-style walk has full flexibility as to the path followed). It is usually best not to plan your precise journey too much or be glued to a map, so that you are free to follow any omens or intuitions, as well as keep your attention primarily on the physical and spiritual landscape you are traversing. If you find yourself at a significant crossroads but are unsure which direction to choose, or at any point where you want the gods' input as to your course, divination is extremely useful.

You can either carry a preferred divinatory system with you, or use items in your environment creatively for this purpose—for instance, marking a stick on one end, spinning it, then following the direction it indicates. If you use a premade system, it should probably be a simple one; something like Tarot involves needlessly complex symbolism when a coin toss could serve just as easily (although you may want to have a more complex system on hand for other uses on your walks). Divination can also be done *before* setting out, to determine a route and/or a destination—a pendulum held over a map can be particularly helpful for this purpose.

In addition to divination, another approach to deciding where you go as you walk is a combination of playfulness and chance (the latter of which, like divination, makes room for the gods to intervene). Follow a bird, or a random pedestrian. Roll a die each time you reach an intersection and assign directions to the point values. Take an entire journey where you only make clockwise turns.

As you walk, pay close attention to all that you perceive with your physical senses (while also, of course, keeping your spiritual awareness tuned in). Note which animals, plants and fungi you encounter, and consider if any gods or spirits you know are associated with them. Keep an eye out for messages from the spirit world, especially those in forms most common to the urban environment, such as billboards, graffiti, and found objects. (One sometimes finds single playing cards discarded on the sidewalk, for instance—these all correspond to Tarot cards and can therefore function in a divinatory capacity.) Listen for *kledones* (overheard snatches of conversation taken as an omen), especially from those people— buskers, the homeless—who are intimately connected to the city streets. Look *up* (something most people fail to do in cities) and look *down* on the ground. Notice the general, and the specific. Fully immerse yourself in your surroundings.

Once you have been taking spirit-walks for awhile, you may want to start assembling a travel kit: a collection of tools and offerings to bring along on your journeys. This is especially true if—as part of a more comprehensive localized spiritual practice—you tend to spend extensive time in ritual or meditation in numinous spots along the way or at your destination. (A smaller kit, pared down to the essentials, could suffice for shorter trips, or even as an everyday accompaniment if you don't own a car or otherwise have cause to walk frequently.)

It can be helpful to have this kit always stocked and assembled, ready to be grabbed at a moment's notice, in case you suddenly get the urge to go on a ramble. The contents will be determined by the specifics of your personal practice, spiritual relationships, and tradition, but it might include such things as:

* tealight candles, incense, and matches or a lighter
* miniature bottles of liquor or other libations
* holy water, or other means of purification
* prayer beads
* paper and pen
* coins, to use as entry "tolls" for places with guardian spirits
* nuts or birdseed, for offerings which can also be safely consumed by wildlife
* honey sticks
* dried herbs and flowers
* red ochre (symbolic blood), blood meal, and/or bone meal, for certain ritual work
* chalk, to make sigils or write prayers
* small glamourbombs (explained below)
* divination methods
* protective talismans
* lancets, if you make blood offerings

* entheogens (obviously these must be used carefully when in public and uncontrolled settings, and there are legal considerations)
* practical items, e.g., food and water, a notebook, binoculars, maps (if necessary), a book (for spending leisure time in a numinous spot), alcohol wipes, waterproof ground cloth, a pocketknife

If you work with the animal dead in the form of remains, you might also consider putting together a kit for handling small roadkill or picking up bones and feathers—including latex gloves, plastic bags, and disinfectant. (Learn and observe all local laws governing collection of roadkill, of course.) Even if you don't collect the physical remains, you might want to bring offerings for any dead animals you encounter. In cities, these are often victims of human activity (mostly from vehicular collision), and it's holy work to make what reparations we can by properly honoring them: burying the body, if possible, or at least carefully moving it off the street or sidewalk, saying a prayer, and leaving flowers, food or another offering to send the spirit on its way.

There are plenty of other offerings you could bring, which will depend on the types of spirits you encounter. Research the traditional offerings made by the animists who lived in your area in the past, and the offerings favored by your religious tradition if you have one. If you study a wide range of animistic cultures, you will find some commonalities that suggest broad guidelines—clean water (especially rainwater or water gathered directly from a natural source) is always welcomed, for instance, and foodstuffs like bread, milk, and honey are enjoyed by many wights. Coins or other precious metals are also common gifts—to make it more special, you can use antique coins, some of which are made of pure silver or copper (favored by some gods and spirits), and/or use metal stamps to emboss short prayers.

Along with a travel kit, you can also make or acquire a few special tools for this practice. While clothing should foremost serve a practical function (especially if walking in inclement weather or through wild areas), having items that double as magical implements is useful. The two most directly related to spirit-walking specifically would be a staff, cane, or walking stick—perhaps adorned with spells and prayers—and a dedicated pair of shoes. The latter should be sturdy and comfortable, but could be given some extra mojo with the addition of charms tied to the laces and/or magical symbols inscribed on the soles. (A particularly appropriate sigil would be the runic Vegvisir [pictured to the right], which prevents the wearer from getting lost— although of course, this might not work for you if you *want* to get a little lost.) The same approach could

be used on a special jacket or hat always worn on your walks.

While most offerings you make during this practice will be small, simple and ephemeral, you may be called to build something a bit more complex and semi-permanent, such as a full shrine, either for a local manifestation of a god, or for powerful spirits of place. This always carries some risk of disappointment, as public spaces are not under your control, and urban areas in particular are used by many kinds of people, not all of whom will understand or respect what you have created. Divination should be done to determine if such a structure is acceptable (considering it may accumulate miasma if touched or destroyed by unsympathetic strangers), and if so, its precise location and design. If constructed, the act itself should be viewed as the offering, with the understanding that it will probably not remain there forever. Still, building a public shrine—and maintaining it as long as it lasts—can be a powerful devotional act. It can also serve as a destination to return to on subsequent walks, aiding in establishing a spot as particularly holy. To minimize the possibility of destruction, consider making something more subtle but still meaningful—a special arrangement of stones, for instance, is sacred in a number of traditions, but may be unnoticed by the casual passerby.

A different way to re-enchant the world on your walks, and one especially suited to the city, is by making and distributing glamourbombs. These are potent intersections of art and magic meant to create doorways for the spirits and thin the veil between here and Elsewhere. They can be as simple as a spell written in chalk on a brick wall, or as elaborate as large, finished artwork intentionally "abandoned" in a public place. When left for other people to find, at least part of the purpose is to act as a magical wake-up call, bringing a sudden awareness of the strange and wonderful spiritual reality all around them. Though if made with proper intention and technique, they should function as magical objects even if unseen by human eyes. The spirits, after all, are always watching, and They appreciate art and beauty as much as anyone.

An easy type of glamourbomb to make and carry with you on walks is the "street oracle." Use a photograph, Tarot or playing card, miniature collage or ATC, or basically any image small and sturdy enough to keep in your pocket. Write a message on it—this could be a line from a song or poem, a favorite quote, or even a random phrase you receive in a spiritually-receptive state. Then leave this card somewhere it will be found—taped to a phone pole, stuck between the slats of a fence, tucked inside a book in the library. Trust that the gods and spirits will lead the right person to the message.

Offerings, shrines and glamourbombs are the things we can leave behind on our walks, but there are also things we can pick up and take with us. Keep an eye out for meaningful items you might encounter—a plant with magical properties, a special feather, a broken piece of jewelry lost by its owner. These things can either be used in later spiritual practice, made into offerings, or kept as mementos of your walks. In many cities, you will also find food freely growing in public spaces but ungathered—blackberries, small, gnarled apples, edible "weeds." These can also be used as offerings, or serve as nourishment as you walk, a way to intimately commune with the city spirits.

Finally, you can create lasting records of your spirit-walks in a variety of ways. Keep a journal. Write poems or prayers to the places you've been. Make drawings (or take artistic photographs, if you can avoid the tempting distraction of an electronic device). Build a shrine in your home out of the special objects found on your walks. Create maps of places where you've met potent wights— either by marking up a printed map, or drawing one from scratch, using your own special place-names and including only what is spiritually significant to you—illustrating a sort of alternate version of your city, thoroughly re-enchanted.

"The alleys become lichways
On foggy city nights like this
And when the traveler is drawn
To ghostly lights, he must resist
Or he will wander endlessly
Inside a maze of neon mist"

– poem written by the author on a spirit-walk

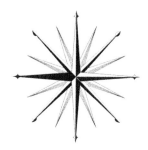

Further Exploration

THE FOLLOWING BOOKS ARE SUGGESTED for further reading on the topics of animism, psychogeography, walking, natural environments, and urban paganism.

The Lost Art of Reading Nature's Signs
    by Tristan Gooley
Urban Habitats
    by C. Philip Wheater
The Wander Society
    by Keri Smith
Psychogeography
    by Merlin Coverley

Wanderlust: A History of Walking
    by Rebecca Solnit
How to Walk
    by Thich Nhat Hanh
Ways to Wander
    by Clare Qualmann and Claire Hind
The Old Ways: A Journey on Foot
    by Robert Macfarlane
Animism: Respecting the Living World
    by Graham Harvey
The Spell of the Sensuous: Perception and Language in a More-Than-Human World
    by David Abram
The Urban Primitive: Paganism in the Concrete Jungle
    by Raven Kaldera and Tannin Schwartzstein

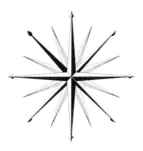

Your Guide

SARAH KATE ISTRA WINTER (AKA DVER) HAS been a polytheist for over 20 years, and an animist since childhood. She first discovered the liminal magic of urban spaces in a hidden alley in Portland, Maine, but only deepened into a full spirit-walking practice after moving across the country and meeting the potent wights of Eugene, Oregon. She has explored the numinous landscape of cities from Athens to London to Boston, but has found a home in the Pacific Northwest, where moss-covered trees line the streets and sturdy rain boots are an indispensible ritual accoutrement.

She is the author of several books on topics

related to devotional polytheism and spirit-work, including *Kharis*, *Komos*, *Dwelling on the Threshold* and *Between the Worlds*, and is also an artist and diviner. She can be found at BirdSpiritLand.com.